CONTENTS

3B

KB101621

I Have a Dance Class

Mini Talk Look and listen.

It's Monday.

Hooray!
I have a dance class today.
I can dance very well.

Great, Lucy!

CHECK 1 a ☐ b ☐ 2 a ☐ b ☐

Practice

A Listen and write the letter. 05   **B** Listen and repeat. 06

> It's Monday. I have an art class today.

Monday

1 an art class ☐

2 a computer class ☐

Tuesday

3 a dance class ☐

Wednesday

4 a ballet class ☐

Thursday

5 a robot class ☐

6 a reading class ☐

Friday

7 a cooking class ☐

8 a badminton class ☐

Listen & Talk

Ⓐ Listen, number, and match. 🎧07

Monday

Tuesday

Wednesday

Thursday

Friday

Saturday

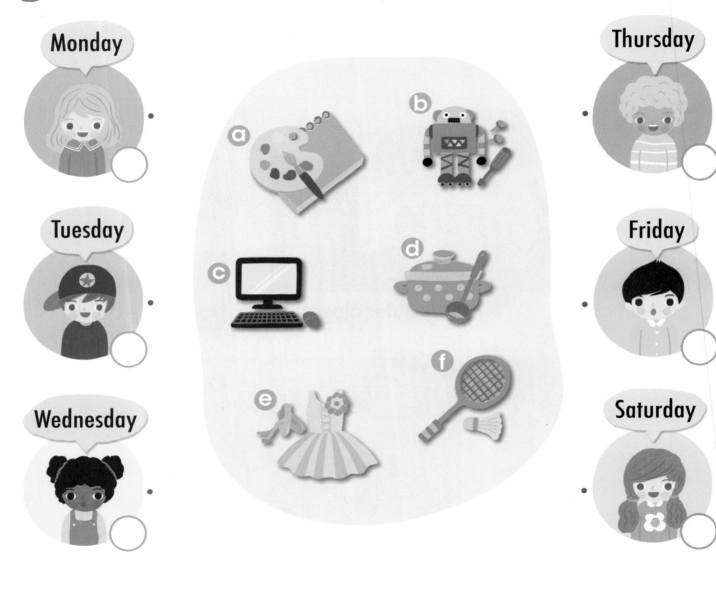

Ⓑ Write and say.

I have a ... class.

1 — I

d_____

2 — We

r_____

3 — They

b_____

Write & Talk

A **Listen, write, and read.** 🎧 08

| art | like | Monday |
| day | cooking | Wednesday |

It's _____.

I have an _____ class today.

Do you _____ art?

Yes, I do.

What _____ is it today?

It's _____.

We have a _____ class today.

That's great! We can eat cookies.

B **Look and write. Then ask and answer.**

Monday   Tuesday   Thursday   Friday

1 A: It's Tuesday. Do you have _____ today?   B: Yes, I do.

2 A: It's Friday. Do you have a computer class today?   B: _____

3 A: It's Monday. Do you have _____ today?   B: Yes, I do.

Story

A Listen, write, and read.

1. What day is it today?
   It's _____.

2. Wow! I have a _____ class today.
   I have an _____ class.

3. Do you have a dance class today?
   No, I _____.

4. I have a _____ class. I can make pizza today.
   That's great.

5. *(no text)*

6. Do you _____ some pizza?
   No, thanks.
   After school

don't   badminton   want   cooking   art   Thursday

B Look and match.

1  •

2  •

3  •

ⓐ • I have a cooking class.

ⓑ • I have a badminton class.

ⓒ • I have an art class.

Challenge

Stick and write. Then ask and answer.

Monday	Tuesday	Wednesday	Thursday	Friday
Sticker		Sticker	Sticker	

 What day is it today?

It's _____.

I have _____ today.

Ⓐ Listen and choose. 🎧11

1
ⓐ
ⓑ
ⓒ

2
ⓐ
ⓑ
ⓒ

Ⓑ Listen and write T or F. 🎧12

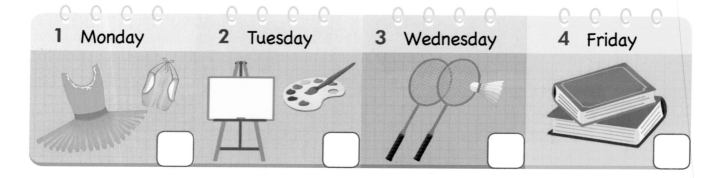

1 Monday   2 Tuesday   3 Wednesday   4 Friday

Ⓒ Listen and match. 🎧13

① ② ③ ④

Monday   Tuesday   Thursday   Sunday

 ⓐ
 ⓑ
 ⓒ
 ⓓ

D Look, write, and circle.

1

Sat.

A: What day is it today?

B: It's _____.

I have a (badminton / dance) class.

2

Wed.

A: What day is it today?

B: It's _____.

We have a (computer / ballet) class.

3

Fri.

A: It's _____.

Do you have a cooking class today?

B: (Yes, I do. / No, I don't.)

E Write and say.

1

It's Monday.

I have _____.

2

It's Thursday.
We _____.

It's Time for School

Mini Talk Look and listen.

It's seven fifty.
It's time for school.

What time is it there?

It's eight fifty.
It's time for bed.

CHECK 1 a ☐ b ☐ 2 a ☐ b ☐

Practice

A Listen and write the letter.  18   **B** Listen and repeat. 19

| What time is it? | It's seven thirty.
It's time for breakfast. |

MY DAY

1 breakfast ☐

2 school ☐

3 class ☐

4 lunch ☐

5 dinner ☐

6 homework ☐

7 bed ☐

Listen & Talk

(A) Listen, write, and match. 🎧 20

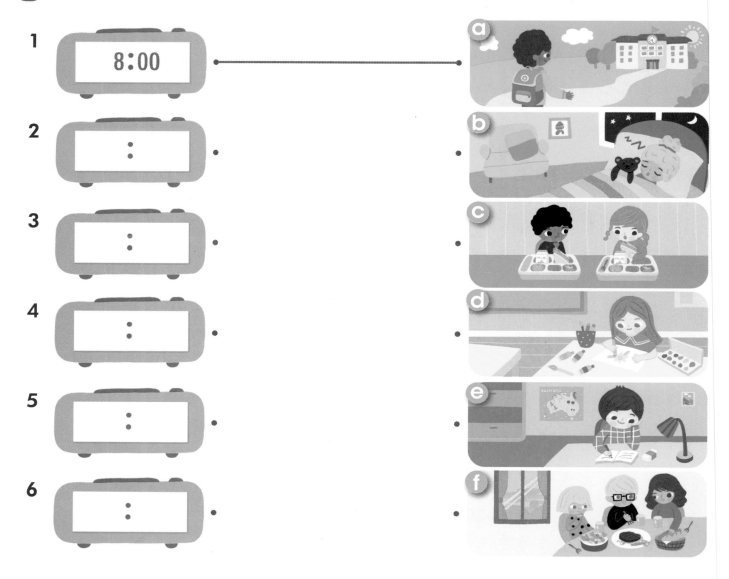

1 8:00

2

3

4

5

6

(B) Write and say.

It's time for ....

1 b_____

2 s_____

3 h_____

Write & Talk

A Listen, write, and read. 21

I'm hungry. What _____ is it?

It's _____ o'clock.

It's time for _____.

Good. Let's go.

It's three _____.

Oh, _____ late.

It's time for a computer _____.

Hurry up!

B Stick and write. Then ask and answer.

dinner   bed   school

1 A: It's eight twenty.

   B: It's time for _____.

2 A: It's six o'clock.

   B: It's time for _____.

3 A: It's nine thirty.

   B: It's time for _____.

Story

Ⓐ Listen, write, and read. ▶ 🎧22

1. It's seven thirty.
   It's time for _____.

   Okay. I want some bread.

2. It's eight o'clock.
   It's time for _____.

   Bye, Eric.

   I _____ dinosaurs.

3. It's _____ an art class.

   I like _____.

5. It's nine fifty.
   It's time for _____.

   Okay. Good night, Mom.

---

like   bed   breakfast   school   time for   art

B Read and match.

What time is it?

1 It's seven thirty. •

2 It's eight o'clock. •

3 It's nine fifty. •

a • It's time for bed.

b • It's time for breakfast.

c • It's time for school.

Challenge

Write and say.

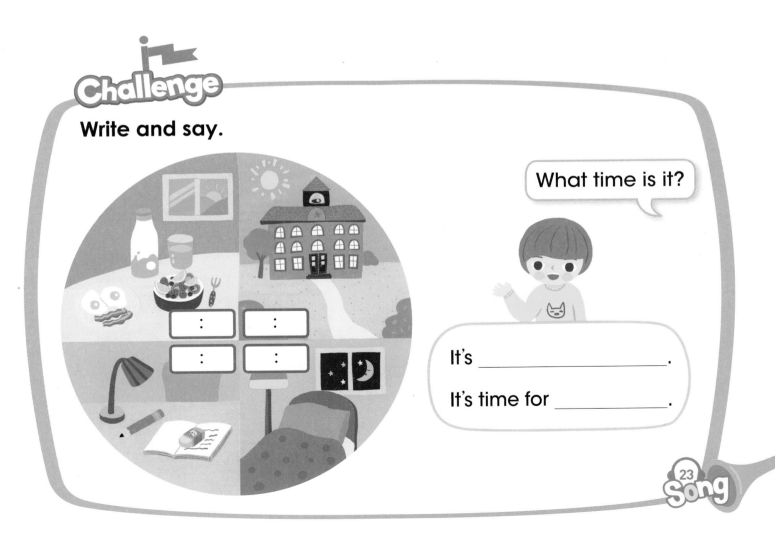

What time is it?

It's _____.

It's time for _____.

Song 23

A Listen and choose. 24

1

ⓐ

ⓑ

ⓒ

2

ⓐ

ⓑ

ⓒ

B Listen and number. 25

C Listen and match. 26

① ② ③ ④

8:00   12:15   4:30   10:20

ⓐ   ⓑ   ⓒ   ⓓ

D Circle, check, and write.

1

A: What time is it?

B: It's (seven o'clock / eight twenty).

It's time for _____.

☐ school   ☐ bed

2

A: It's (twelve thirty / twelve fifty).

B: Oh, it's time for _____.

☐ homework   ☐ lunch

3

A: It's (ten o'clock / eleven o'clock).

It's time for _____.

☐ an art class   ☐ breakfast

B: I like art.

E Write and say.

1

What time is it?

It's seven ten.

_____

2

What time is it?

_____

It's time for bed.

A Look and write.

art   robot   cooking   dance   badminton

1 a _____ class

2 an _____ class

3 a _____ class

4 a _____ class

5 a _____ class

school   dinner   bed
breakfast   class

6 time for _____

7 time for _____

8 time for _____

9 time for _____

10 time for _____

B **Look and match.**

What day is it today?

1 It's Friday. •
2 It's Wednesday. •
3 It's Monday. •

a • I have a ballet class today.

b • I have a computer class today.

c • I have a reading class today.

C **Follow and write.**

What time is it?

1 It's seven forty.

2 It's nine fifty.

3 It's twelve thirty.

It's time for _____.

It's time for _____.

It's time for _____.

homework   lunch   bed

How Much Is It?

Mini Talk Look and listen.

I like this hair band. How much is it?

It's two dollars.

Okay. I'll take it.

Thank you.

CHECK 1 a b 2 a b

20

Practice

A Listen and write the letter. 🎧31   **B** Listen and repeat. 🎧32

How much is the fan?

Yard Sale

1 fan ☐ — $2

2 hair band ☐ — $3

3 mask ☐ — $4

4 storybook ☐ — $5

5 pencil case ☐ — $6

6 teddy bear ☐ — $7

7 board game ☐ — $8

8 soccer ball ☐ — $9

It's two dollars.

Listen & Talk

A Listen, number, and match. 🎧 33

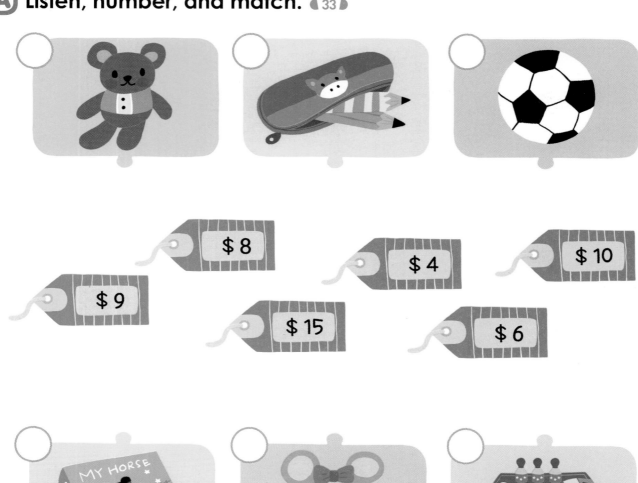

  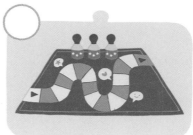

B Write and say.

The ~ is ... dollars.

1

$7

f_____

2

$15

m_____

3

$20

t_____

Write & Talk

A Listen, write, and read. 🎧 34

eight	help	soccer ball
three	much	pencil case

- Can I _____ you?
- Yes, please.

  How much is the _____?
- It's _____ dollars.

- I want this _____.

  How _____ is it?
- It's _____ dollars.
- Here you are.

B Look and write. Then ask and answer.

kite
jump rope
teddy bear

1   A: How much is the _____?

   B: It's _____ dollars.

2   A: How much is the _____?

   B: It's _____ dollars.

3   A: How much is the _____?

   B: It's _____ _____.

Story

A Listen, write, and read. ▶ 🎧35

1

I like this _____.
It's three dollars.

$3

2

I want this _____.
_____ is it?

It's five dollars.

3

How much is the _____?

It's four dollars.

4

$3 + $5 + $4 = $12

We have ten dollars.

5

Look! It's two dollars.

50% Sale

That's great!

6

_____ you are.

Thank you.

$10

| Here | storybook | board game | How much | teddy bear |

24

B Match and write.

1

    •   • ⓐ The board game is _____ dollars.

2

    •   • ⓑ The _____ is two dollars.

3

    •   • ⓒ The teddy bear is _____ dollars.

Challenge

Check and write.

☐ ········ $5

☐  ········ $2

☐ ········ $7

☐ ········ $15

I want this _____.

It's _____ dollars.

36 Song

Check-Up

A Listen and number. 🎧37

B Listen, match, and choose. 🎧38

①   ②   ③

ⓐ ⓑ

ⓐ ⓑ

ⓐ ⓑ

C Listen and write T or F. 🎧39

1

2

3

26

D Look, circle, and write.

1

The _____ is three dollars.
(fan / storybook)
I like it.

2

A: How much is the _____?
(soccer ball / mask)
B: It's _____ dollars.

3

A: I like this _____.
(teddy bear / storybook)
How much is it?
B: It's _____.

E Write and say.

1

How much is the hair band?

$5

2

It's seven dollars.

Mini Talk Look and listen. ▶ 🎧42

Okay.

Don't push, Kevin. Line up, please.

Sit down, please.

Okay. I'm sorry.

🎧43 CHECK 1 a ☐ b ☐ 2 a ☐ b ☐

28

Practice

A Listen and write the letter. 🎧 44   **B** Listen and repeat. 🎧 45

Line up.	Okay.

be quiet ☐

1 line up ☐

5 take out the trash ☐

4 pick up the trash ☐

3 wash your hands ☐

put the bottles here ☐

6

7 put the paper here ☐

8 put the cans here ☐

Listen & Talk

A Listen and number. 🎧 46

B Write and say.

..., please.

1

put the _____s here

2

_____ your hands

3

_____ up the trash

Write & Talk

A Listen, write, and read. 🎧47

Be quiet	talk
Pick up	Don't

_____ do that.

_____ the trash, please.

Okay. I'm sorry.

Don't _____.

_____, please.

Okay. I'm sorry.

B Stick and write. Then say.

paper	bottles	cans

1 Put the _____ here.

2 Put the _____ here.   3 Put the _____ here.

A Listen, write, and read. ▶ 🎧 48

Be quiet   Where   Pick up   Line up   lunch

B Read and check.

1

☐ Line up, please.

☐ Don't push, please.

2

☐ Wash your hands, please.

☐ Be quiet, please.

3

☐ Pick up the trash, please.

☐ Put the bottles here, please.

Challenge

Circle the two people and write.

• _____, please.

• _____, please.

Check-Up

A Listen and number. 🎧50

B Listen and match. 🎧51

1   2   3   4

C Listen and choose. 🎧52

1
    a   b

2
    a   b

3
    a   b

D Look, circle, and write.

1

A: Put the _____ here.
(cans / paper)
B: Okay.

2

A: It's time for lunch.
_____, please.
(Line up / Wash your hands)
B: Okay.

3

A: Don't do that. _____
(Put the cans here. / Pick up the trash.)
B: Oh, I'm sorry.

E Write and say.

1

Okay.

2

Oh, I'm sorry.

A Match and write.

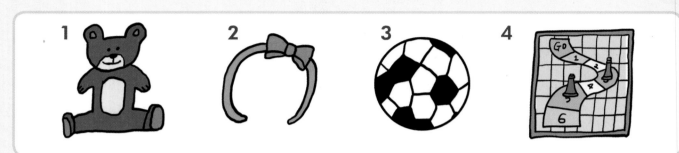

1   teddy •   • ball   _____

2   hair •   • game   _____

3   soccer •   • bear   _____

4   board •   • band   _____

B Look, choose, and write.   cans   paper   pick up   take out

1   put the _____ here   2   put the _____ here

3   _____ the trash   4   _____ the trash

C Read and write the price.

A: How much is the mask?

B: It's nine dollars.

A: How much is the storybook?

B: It's ten dollars.

A: How much is the fan?

B: It's fifteen dollars.

A: How much is the pencil case?

B: It's three dollars.

D Look, choose, and write.

1

A: _____

B: Okay.

2

A: _____

B: Okay.

3

A: _____

B: Oh, I'm sorry.

| Be quiet, please. | Line up, please. | Wash your hands. |

This Hat Is Too Big

Mini Talk Look and listen. ▶ 🎧55

Practice

A Listen and write the letter. 🎧 57   **B** Listen and repeat. 🎧 58

This pencil is too short. I can't write.	These shoes are too big. I can't run.

1 pencil

short / write ☐

2 bed

small / sleep ☐

3 tea

hot / drink it ☐

4 shoes

big / run ☐

5 pants

long / walk ☐

6 cookies

hard / eat them ☐

Listen & Talk

A Listen and number. 🎧59

B Write and say.

> This ~ is too .... / These ~ are too ....

1
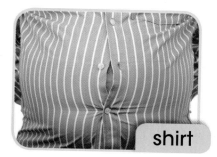
shirt

_____

2

hat

_____

3

pants

_____

Write & Talk

A Listen, write, and read. 🎧 60

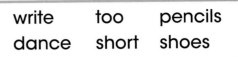

write	too	pencils
dance	short	shoes

This pencil is too _____.

I can't _____.

I have two _____.

Here you are.

These shoes are _____ small.

I can't _____.

That's too bad.

You need new _____.

B Match and write. Then say.

long	small	hot
sleep	drink	walk

1

2

3

a This bed is too _____.

I can't _____.

b This milk is too _____.

I can't _____ it.

c These pants are too _____.

I can't _____.

Story

A Listen, write, and read. ▶ 🎧 61

1. This pencil is too _____.
   I can't _____.

2. I'm _____.

3. These cookies are _____ hard.
   I can't eat them.

4. I'm sleepy.

5. This _____ is too small.
   I can't _____.

6. Goodbye, Bear!

| too | hungry | short | bed | write | sleep |

B Read, match, and write.

1

ⓐ These cookies are too _____.

I can't eat them.

2

ⓑ This pencil is too _____.

I can't write.

3

ⓒ This bed is too _____.

I can't sleep.

Challenge

Find the two differences. Then write about Ⓑ.

A   B

Ⓑ 1 This _____ is too _____.

2 These _____ are too _____.

Check-Up

A Listen and choose. 🎧63

1

ⓐ ⓑ

2

ⓐ ⓑ

3

ⓐ ⓑ

B Listen and circle T or F. 🎧64

1

T
F

2

T
F

3

T
F

4

T
F

C Listen, number, and circle. 🎧65

long   short

small   hard

small   big

D Look, write, and circle.

big   hard   short

1

This bed is too _____.

I can't (eat / sleep).

2

These shoes are too _____.

I can't (drink / run).

3

This pencil is too _____.

I can't (write / see).

E Write and say.

1

_____
I can't eat it.

2

_____
I can't walk.

What Are You Doing?

Mini Talk Look and listen. ▶ 🎧68

CHECK 69 1 a ☐ b ☐ 2 a ☐ b ☐

Practice

A Listen and write the letter. 🎧 70

B Listen and repeat. 🎧 71

| What are you doing? | I'm singing. |

1 singing ☐

2 drawing ☐

3 studying ☐

4 cooking ☐

5 eating lunch ☐

6 watching TV ☐

7 playing the piano ☐

8 playing the violin ☐

Listen & Talk

A Listen and choose. 🎧72

1

2

3

4

5

6

B Write and say.

I'm ....

1

_____ the violin

2

_____ TV

3

_____ lunch

Write & Talk

A Listen, write, and read. 🎧73

fly	cooking	doing
like	studying	busy

What are you _____, Mom?

I'm _____.

Do you _____ carrots?

Sure.

Let's _____ a kite.

Sorry, I can't. I'm _____.

What are you doing?

I'm _____.

B Look and write. Then ask and answer.

singing   drawing
playing the piano

1   A: What are you doing?

    B: I'm _____.

2   A: What are you doing?

    B: I'm _____.

3   A: What are you doing?

    B: I'm _____.

Story

A Listen, write, and read. 74

1. What are you doing?
   I'm _____ TV.

2. What are you doing?
   I'm _____.

3. _____ are you doing?
   I'm _____ the piano.

4. Oh, I'm _____.

5. She's _____ the living room.

6. Happy birthday!
   Wow! Thank you.

sad   playing   watching   cooking   in   What

B **Read and match.**

1

2

3

What are you doing?

ⓐ I'm playing the piano.

ⓑ I'm cooking.

ⓒ I'm watching TV.

What are you doing?

Challenge

Guess and write.

1

➡ _____

2

➡ _____

75 Song

(A) Listen and write T or F. 🎧76

1

2

3

(B) Listen and choose. 🎧77

1

ⓐ ⓑ

2

ⓐ ⓑ

3

ⓐ ⓑ

(C) Listen and number. 🎧78

D Look, check, and write.

1

A: What are you doing?

B: I'm _____.

☐ eating lunch ☐ watching TV

2

A: I'm _____. Can you help me?

☐ drawing ☐ singing

B: Sure.

3

A: Let's play basketball.

B: Sorry, I can't. _____

☐ I'm cooking. ☐ I'm studying.

E Write and say.

1

What are you doing?

2

What are you doing?

Review 3

A **Look and circle.**

1

eat

sleep

2

walk

cook

3

draw

drink

4

write

run

5

singing

watching

6

sleeping

cooking

7

playing

studying

8

eating

drawing

B **Look and write.**

| hard | hot | small | run | drink | eat |

1 This tea is too _____. I can't _____ it.

2 These cookies are too _____. I can't _____ them.

3 These shoes are too _____. I can't _____.

C **Look and number.**

What are you doing?

◯ I'm watching TV.   ◯ I'm eating lunch.

◯ I'm playing the piano.   ◯ I'm playing the violin.

Mini Talk Look and listen. ▶ 🎧 81

Practice

A Listen and write the letter. 83   **B** Listen and repeat. 84

| What is he/she doing? | He's/She's making dinner. |

1 making dinner ☐

dancing ☐

2 washing the dishes ☐

3 cleaning the house ☐

4

5 drinking water ☐

6 sleeping ☐

7 making a robot ☐

8 reading a book ☐

Listen & Talk

Ⓐ Listen and number. 🎧 85

Ⓑ Write and say.

> He's/She's ....

1

_____ the dishes

2

_____ a book

3

_____ a robot

Write & Talk

A Listen, write, and read. 🎧86

He's	in	doing
I'm	are	making

1

👧 What _____ you doing?

👧 _____ drawing.

👦 What is Jake doing?

👧 _____ sleeping.

2

👵 Where is Dan?

👩 He's _____ the yard.

👵 What is he _____?

👩 He's _____ a snowman.

B Match and write. Then ask and answer.

> Where is he/she?
>
> What is he/she doing?

1 [picture]

2 [picture]

3 [picture]

ⓐ She's in the kitchen.

She's _____.

ⓑ He's in the living room.

He's _____.

ⓒ She's in the bedroom.

She's _____.

| reading a book | washing the dishes | cleaning the house |

A Listen, write, and read. ▶ 🎧 87

1
Where is Mom?

She's _____ the camping car.

2
What are _____ doing, Mom?

I'm _____ the dishes.

3
What is Dad doing?

He's _____ dinner.

4
What is Amy doing?

_____ playing with Max.

5
Amy, it's time _____ dinner. Come here.

6
Max, you're not Amy.

| you | She's | washing | for | making | in |

B Read and match.

1

2

3

ⓐ She's playing with Max.

ⓑ He's making dinner.

ⓒ She's washing the dishes.

Challenge

Stick and write. Then ask and answer.

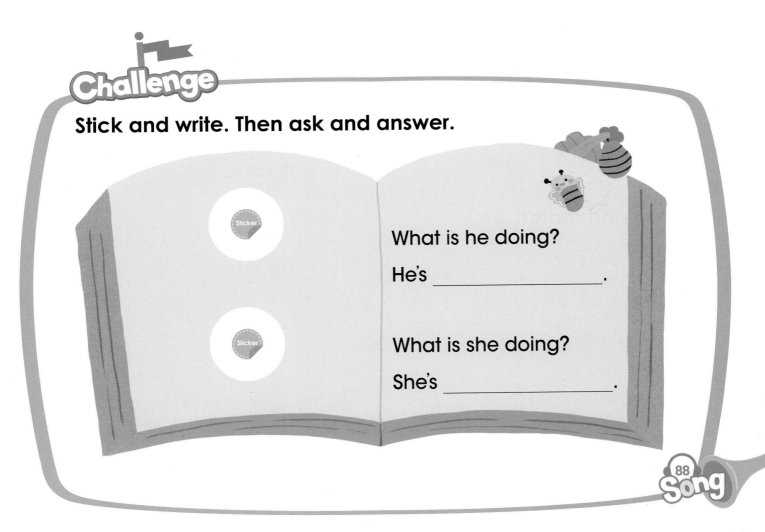

Sticker

Sticker

What is he doing?

He's _____.

What is she doing?

She's _____.

88 Song

Check-Up

Ⓐ Listen and write T or F. 🎧89

1

2

3

Ⓑ Listen and choose. 🎧90

1

ⓐ ⓑ

2

ⓐ ⓑ

3

ⓐ ⓑ

Ⓒ Listen and match. 🎧91

① ② ③ ④

ⓐ  ⓑ  ⓒ  ⓓ

D Circle, choose, and write.

sleeping   reading a book
washing the dishes

1

A: What is (he / she) doing?

B: (He's / She's) _____.

2

A: Dad is in the kitchen.

B: What is (he / she) doing?

A: (He's / She's) _____.

3

A: Where is your sister?

B: (He's / She's) in the living room.

(He's / She's) _____.

E Write and say.

1

What is she doing?

2

What is he doing?

He's Wearing a Jacket

Mini Talk Look and listen. ▶ 🎧94

I can't see you.
What are you wearing?

I'm wearing a dress.

Tony is wearing a jacket.

Oh, I see you.

🎧95
CHECK   1 ⓐ [ ] ⓑ [ ]   2 ⓐ [ ] ⓑ [ ]

Practice

A Listen and write the letter. 🎧 96   **B** Listen and repeat. 🎧 97

| What is he/she wearing? | He's/She's wearing a sweater. |

a sweater ☐

a skirt ☐

a blouse ☐

a dress ☐

a jacket ☐

a T-shirt ☐

pants ☐

a shirt ☐

Listen & Talk

A Listen and match. 🎧98

B Write and say.

> He/She's wearing a ....

1 red _____

2 blue _____

3 yellow _____

Write & Talk

A Listen, write, and read. 🎧99

blouse	she	jacket
sweater	skirt	wearing

What are you _____?

I'm wearing a _____.

It's windy today.

Put on your _____, too.

That's my mom.

What is _____ wearing?

She's wearing a white_____

and a pink _____.

B Look and write. Then ask and answer.

What are you wearing?

1 I'm wearing a _____ _____.

2 I'm wearing a _____ _____.

3 I'm wearing a _____ _____.

4 I'm wearing _____ _____.

T-shirt	cap	jacket	pants

A Listen, write, and read. 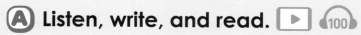 100

1. What is he _____?

   He's wearing a red jacket.

2. _____ wearing red pants, too.

3. Is he a _____?

   Yes, he is.

4. What is she wearing?

   _____ wearing a white jacket.

5. No, she isn't. She's wearing a _____ hat, too.

   Is she a doctor?

6. Is she a _____?

   Yes, she is.

cook   firefighter   white   wearing   He's   She's

B Read and check.

What is he wearing?

☐ He's wearing a blue cap.

☐ He's wearing a red jacket.

☐ He's wearing red pants.

What is she wearing?

☐ She's wearing a white jacket.

☐ She's wearing a yellow skirt.

☐ She's wearing a white hat.

Stick and write. Then say.

He's wearing _____

and _____.

She's wearing _____

and _____.

Check-Up

A Listen and match. 🎧102

1  2  3  4

ⓐ 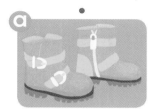 ⓑ  ⓒ  ⓓ

B Listen and write T or F. 🎧103

C Listen and choose. 🎧104

1

2

70

D Look, check, and write.

1

A: What are you wearing?

B: I'm wearing _____.

☐ a green T-shirt ☐ a green jacket

2

A: What is she wearing?

B: She's wearing _____.

☐ a yellow dress ☐ a yellow sweater

3

A: He's wearing a blue hat and _____.

☐ a blue skirt ☐ a blue shirt

B: He's a police officer.

E Write and say.

1

What are you wearing?

2

What is she wearing?

Ⓐ Look and number.

◯ reading a book

◯ drinking water

◯ making a robot

◯ cleaning the house

◯ a shirt

◯ a sweater

◯ a dress

◯ pants

B Look and choose.

What is he/she doing?

1 **a** He's drawing.
   b He's dancing.

2 **a** She's singing.
   b She's sleeping.

3 **a** She's making dinner.
   b She's eating lunch.

4 **a** He's washing the dishes.
   b He's drinking juice.

C Look, circle, and write.

What is he/she wearing?

1 He's wearing a (green / blue) _____.

2 She's wearing a (pink / red) _____.

3 He's wearing a (black / brown) _____.

4 She's wearing a (yellow / white) _____.

jacket
T-shirt
skirt
blouse

Songs

Unit 1 **I Have a Cooking Class Today**

It's Monday.

I have a cooking class today.

I have a robot class today.

   It's Friday.

   We have a reading class today.

   We have an art class today.

   We like art. Yeah!

Unit 2 **It's Time for School**

It's eight o'clock.

It's time for school. Let's go!

   It's twelve thirty.

   It's time for lunch. Let's eat!

It's nine thirty.

It's time for bed. Good night!

Unit 3 **How Much Is the Mask?**

How much is the mask?

   It's two dollars.

How much is the storybook?

   It's five dollars.

How much is the soccer ball?

   It's ten dollars.

Okay. I'll take it.

Unit 4 **Line Up, Please**

Line up. Line up, please.

   Oh, I'm sorry.

Pick up the trash.

Pick up the trash, please.

   Okay.

Be quiet. Be quiet, please.

   Oh, I'm sorry.

Unit 5 This Pencil Is Too Short

This pencil is too short.

I can't write. Oh, no!

   This bed is too small.

   I can't sleep. Oh, no!

These shoes are too big.

I can't walk. Oh, no!

Unit 6 What Are You Doing? 75

What are you doing?

   Cooking, cooking. I'm cooking.

   Singing, singing. I'm singing.

What are you doing?

   Drawing, drawing. I'm drawing.

   Watching, watching. I'm watching

   TV.

Unit 7 She's Sleeping

What is he doing?

What is he doing?

   He's dancing. Wow!

What is she doing?

What is she doing?

   She's sleeping.

What are you doing?

What are you doing?

   I'm reading a book. Shh!

Unit 8 He's Wearing a Green T-shirt 101

What is he wearing?

   He's wearing a green T-shirt.

   He's wearing blue pants.

Oh, cool! He's cool!

What is she wearing?

   She's wearing a red blouse.

   She's wearing a yellow skirt.

Oh, cool! She's cool!

A Listen and repeat. Then read. 🎧 105

1 oo → cool

2 oo → moon

3 oo → roof

4 o-e → hole

5 o-e → rope

6 o-e → stone

B Listen and check. 🎧 106

1
☐ rope
☐ roof

2
☐ hole
☐ cool

3
☐ stone
☐ moon

4
☐ moon
☐ rope

C Circle and match.

1

oo | o-e

2

oo | o-e

3

oo | o-e

cool

hole

stone

Phonics ②

A Listen and repeat. Then read. 107

sm
sn
sw

1 sm → smell

2 sm → smile

3 sn → snail

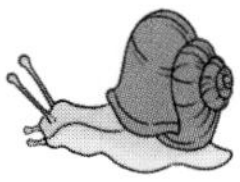

4 sn → snake

5 sw → swing

6 sw → sweet

B Listen and circle. 108

1 swing
smile

2 sweet
snail

3 smell
swing

4 smile
snake

C Match and write.

1

_____ _____ing

2

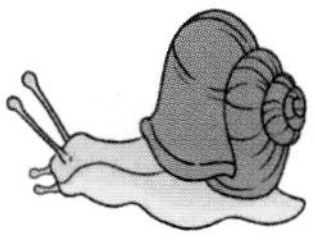

_____ _____ell

3

_____ _____ail

Ⓐ Listen and repeat. Then read. 🎧109

st
sp
sk

1 st → stop

2 st → stove

3 sp → spot

4 sp → spoon

5 sk → sky

6 sk → skate

Ⓑ Listen and check. 🎧110

1 ☐ skate
☐ stove

2 ☐ stop
☐ spot

3 ☐ stove
☐ sky

4 ☐ spoon
☐ skate

Ⓒ Circle and write.

1

| sk | sp |

_____y

2

| st | sk |

_____op

3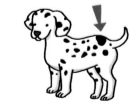

| st | sp |

_____ot

Ⓐ Listen, circle, and write. 🎧111

1 sw sn sm   2 st sn sk   3 sk st sw   4 sm sp sn

___ ___ail   ___ ___y   ___ ___op   ___ ___ile

Ⓑ Listen, circle, and match. 🎧112

1 smell   2 snake   3 skate   4 stove

   swing   skate   spot   spoon

   •   •   •   •

   •   •   •   •

Ⓒ Check and write.

1 ☐ sn   2 ☐ sk   3 ☐ sp
   ☐ sw   ☐ st   ☐ sm

___ ___eet   ___ ___ove   ___ ___ell

A Listen and repeat. Then read. 113

ar
or

1 ar → car

2 ar → star

3 ar → park

4 or → corn

5 or → fork

6 or → horse

B Listen and check. 114

1
☐ park
☐ fork

2
☐ corn
☐ car

3
☐ horse
☐ park

4
☐ fork
☐ star

C Match and write.

1

•
• h___ ___se

2

•
• f___ ___k

3

•
• c___ ___

A Listen and repeat. Then read. 🎧115

ir er ur

1 ir → girl

2 ir → bird

3 er → germ

4 er → serve

5 ur → turtle

6 ur → purple

B Listen and circle. 🎧116

1 germ   bird   turtle

2 serve   girl   purple

3 germ   girl   purple

4 germ   girl   turtle

C Circle and write.

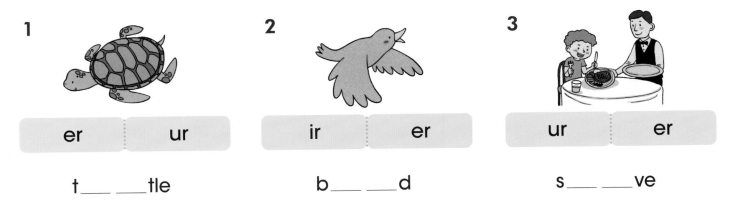

1 er   ur   t___ ___tle

2 ir   er   b___ ___d

3 ur   er   s___ ___ve

A Listen and repeat. Then read.  117

air
ear

1 air → hair

2 air → chair

3 air → stair

4 ear → ear

5 ear → hear

6 ear → near

B Listen and check. 118

1
☐ ear
☐ stair

2
☐ hear
☐ hair

3
☐ stair
☐ hear

4
☐ near
☐ hair

C Match and write.

1   •   • st____ ____ ____

2    •   • h____ ____ ____

3 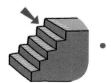   •   • ch____ ____ ____

Ⓐ Listen, circle, and write. 🎧119

1 | air ar ur   **2** | ear or er   **3** | ir ur er   **4** | ar er or

st_____   n_____   t_____tle   s_____ve

Ⓑ Listen, circle, and match. 🎧120

1 | corn   **2** | horse   **3** | bird   **4** | germ

    park   hear   ear   girl

Ⓒ Check and write.

1   ☐ or   **2**   ☐ er   **3**   ☐ ear
    ☐ ar   ☐ ur   ☐ air

f___ ___k   p___ ___ple   h___ ___ ___

Word List 3B

Unit 1   I Have a Dance Class

art _____

badminton _____

ballet _____

class _____

computer _____

cooking _____

dance _____

day _____

reading _____

robot _____

today _____

Unit 2   It's Time for School

bed _____

breakfast _____

class _____

dinner _____

homework _____

hungry _____

hurry up _____

late _____

lunch _____

school _____

sleepy _____

time for _____

Unit 3   How Much Is It?

board game _____

dollar _____

fan _____

hair band _____

how much _____

jump rope _____

mask _____

pencil case _____

soccer ball _____

storybook _____

take _____

teddy bear _____

want _____

Unit 4   Line Up, Please

be quiet _____

don't _____

line up _____

pick up the trash _____

please _____

put the bottles here _____

put the cans here _____

put the paper here _____

take out the trash _____

wash your hands _____

Unit 5 This Hat Is Too Big

cold _____

drink _____

eat _____

hard _____

hot _____

long _____

need _____

new _____

run _____

short _____

sleep _____

walk _____

write _____

Unit 6 What Are You Doing?

cooking _____

doing _____

drawing _____

eating lunch _____

help _____

living room _____

playing the piano _____

playing the violin _____

singing _____

studying _____

watching TV _____

Unit 7 She's Sleeping

bathroom _____

cleaning the house _____

dancing _____

drinking water _____

kitchen _____

making a robot _____

making dinner _____

reading a book _____

sleeping _____

washing the dishes _____

yard _____

Unit 8 He's Wearing a Jacket

blouse _____

boots _____

dress _____

firefighter _____

jacket _____

pants _____

police officer _____

shirt _____

shorts _____

skirt _____

sweater _____

T-shirt _____

wearing _____

Syllabus 3B

Unit 1   I Have a Dance Class

Structures	Vocabulary		Phonics

• What day is it today?
 	
  It's Monday.
• I have an art class today.
• Do you have a dance class today?
 	
  Yes, I do. / No, I don't.
	art
	computer
	dance
	ballet
	robot
		reading
		cooking
		badminton
		class
		today
			Long Vowels
			
			oo, o-e

Unit 2   It's Time for School

Structures	Vocabulary		Phonics

• What time is it?
 	
  It's seven thirty.
• It's time for breakfast.
 	
  It's time for a computer class.
• Hurry up!
	breakfast
	school
	class
	lunch
	dinner
		homework
		bed
		time for
		hungry
		sleepy
			Consonant Blends
			
			sm, sn, sw

Review 1			

Unit 3   How Much Is It?

Structures	Vocabulary		Phonics
• I like/want this hair band. • How much is the fan? It's two dollars. • Can I help you? - Yes, please. • I'll take it. • Here you are.	fan hair band mask storybook pencil case teddy bear	board game soccer ball kite jump rope dollar	Consonant Blends st, sp, sk

Unit 4   Line Up, Please

Structures	Vocabulary		Phonics

• Line up, please.
 	
  Okay.
 	
  Okay. I'm sorry.
• Don't push.
 	
  Don't do that.
	line up
	be quiet
	wash your hands
	pick up the trash
	take out the trash
		put the bottles here
		put the paper here
		put the cans here
		please
			Review: Consonant Blends
			
			sm, sn, sw, st, sp, sk

Review 2			

Unit 5 This Hat Is Too Big

Structures	Vocabulary		Phonics
• This hat is too big.	write	hard	R-controlled Vowels
I can't see.	sleep	short / long	ar, or
• These shoes are too small.	drink	hot / cold	
I can't run.	run	big / small	
• That's too bad.	walk		
• You need new shoes.	eat		

Unit 6 What Are You Doing?

Structures	Vocabulary		Phonics
• What are you doing?	singing	watching TV	R-controlled Vowels
I'm drawing.	drawing	playing the piano	ir, er, ur
• Can you help me? - Sure.	studying	playing the violin	
• Where are you?	cooking		
I'm in the living room.	eating lunch		
Review 3			

Unit 7 She's Sleeping

Structures	Vocabulary		Phonics
• What is he/she doing?	dancing	drinking water	R-controlled Vowels
He's/She's making dinner.	sleeping	making a robot	air, ear
• Where is Dad/Mom?	making dinner	reading a book	
He's/She's in the kitchen.	washing the dishes	making a snowman	
	cleaning the house	playing with Max	

Unit 8 He's Wearing a Jacket

Structures	Vocabulary		Phonics
• What are you wearing?	a sweater	a shirt	Review: R-controlled Vowels
I'm wearing a yellow dress.	a skirt	a cap	
• What is he/she wearing?	a blouse	pants	ar, or, ir, er, ur, air, ear
He's/She's wearing blue pants.	a dress	shorts	
• Put on your jacket.	a T-shirt	boots	
	a jacket	wearing	
Review 4			

Midterm TEST 3B

Institute _____

Name _____

Score _____ /100

[1-2] Listen and choose.
다음을 듣고 알맞은 그림을 고르세요.

1 ⓐ  ⓑ

ⓒ  ⓓ

2 ⓐ  ⓑ

ⓒ  ⓓ

---

3 Listen and choose.
다음을 듣고 그림에 알맞은 것을 고르세요.

$5

ⓐ   ⓑ   ⓒ   ⓓ

[4-5] Listen and mark O or X.
다음을 듣고 그림과 일치하면 ○ 표, 일치하지 않으면 X 표를 하세요.

4    **5**

(   )   (   )

[6-7] Listen and choose.
다음을 듣고 그림에 알맞은 응답을 고르세요.

6

ⓐ   ⓑ   ⓒ   ⓓ

7

ⓐ   ⓑ   ⓒ   ⓓ

---

8 Listen and choose.
대화를 듣고 알맞은 그림을 고르세요.

ⓐ  ⓑ

ⓒ  ⓓ

[9-10] Listen and choose.
다음을 듣고 알맞은 응답을 고르세요.

9 ⓐ That's great. ⓑ No, thanks.

ⓒ Okay. I'm sorry. ⓓ Me, too.

10 ⓐ It's five o'clock. ⓑ It's Monday.

ⓒ It's six dollars. ⓓ It's in the box.

11 Read and choose.
다음을 읽고 알맞은 그림을 고르세요.

Pick up the trash.

ⓐ

ⓑ

ⓒ

ⓓ

[12-13] Look and choose.
그림을 보고 알맞은 것을 고르세요.

12

ⓐ We have a cooking class today.
ⓑ We have an art class today.
ⓒ We have a ballet class today.
ⓓ We have a computer class today.

13

ⓐ The mask is two dollars.
ⓑ The storybook is three dollars.
ⓒ The fan is four dollars.
ⓓ The board game is five dollars.

[14-15] Unscramble and write.
단어를 바르게 배열하여 문장을 쓰세요.

14
_____
(time / for / It's / dinner / .)

15
_____
(a / class / . / have / reading / I)

16 Read and choose.
대화를 읽고 빈칸에 알맞은 것을 고르세요.

A: What day is it?
B: It's _____.

ⓐ good
ⓑ a fan
ⓒ Sunday
ⓓ one o'clock

[17-18] Read and choose.
대화를 읽고 빈칸에 알맞은 것을 고르세요.

17
A: It's ten twenty. _____
B: Okay. Good night.

ⓐ It's time for bed.
ⓑ It's time for school.
ⓒ It's time for lunch.
ⓓ It's time for class.

18
A: I like this teddy bear. _____
B: It's nine dollars.

ⓐ What time is it?
ⓑ How much is it?
ⓒ How many bears?
ⓓ What do you like?

[19-20] Look and write.
그림을 보고 대화의 빈칸에 알맞은 말을 쓰세요.

19

A: It's _____.
B: I have a _____ class today.

20

A: _____ your _____, please.
B: Okay.

Final TEST 3B

Institute

Name

Score   /100

[1-2] Listen and choose.
다음을 듣고 알맞은 그림을 고르세요.

1 ⓐ  ⓑ

ⓒ  ⓓ

2 ⓐ  ⓑ

ⓒ  ⓓ

3 Listen and choose.
다음을 듣고 그림에 알맞은 것을 고르세요.

ⓐ   ⓑ   ⓒ   ⓓ

[4-5] Listen and mark O or X.
다음을 듣고 그림과 일치하면 ○ 표, 일치하지 않으면 X 표를 하세요.

4  **5**

(   )   (   )

[6-7] Listen and choose.
다음을 듣고 그림에 알맞은 응답을 고르세요.

6

ⓐ   ⓑ   ⓒ   ⓓ

7

ⓐ   ⓑ   ⓒ   ⓓ

8 Listen and choose.
대화를 듣고 알맞은 그림을 고르세요.

ⓐ  ⓑ

ⓒ  ⓓ

[9-10] Listen and choose.
다음을 듣고 알맞은 응답을 고르세요.

9 ⓐ I'm playing the piano.

ⓑ He's playing the violin.

ⓒ I'm wearing red pants.

ⓓ He's wearing blue pants.

10 ⓐ I'm wearing a black dress.

ⓑ He's wearing a black jacket.

ⓒ She's making a robot.

ⓓ He's making dinner.

11 Read and choose.
다음을 읽고 알맞은 그림을 고르세요.

She's washing the dishes.

ⓐ    ⓑ

ⓒ    ⓓ

[12-13] Look and choose.
그림을 보고 알맞은 것을 고르세요.

12

ⓐ He's wearing a yellow sweater.

ⓑ He's wearing blue shorts.

ⓒ She's wearing a yellow dress.

ⓓ She's wearing a blue blouse.

13

ⓐ This bed is too hard.

ⓑ This hat is too big.

ⓒ These shoes are too small.

ⓓ These pants are too long.

[14-15] Unscramble and write.
단어를 바르게 배열하여 문장을 쓰세요.

14
_____

(the / I'm / violin / playing / .)

15
_____

(skirt / wearing / . / She's / a / red)

16 Read and choose.
다음을 읽고 빈칸에 알맞은 것을 고르세요.

This pencil is too short.

I can't _____.

ⓐ eat   ⓑ run   ⓒ see   ⓓ write

[17-18] Read and choose.
대화를 읽고 빈칸에 알맞은 것을 고르세요.

17

A: What are you doing?

B: _____

ⓐ I'm studying.   ⓑ He's dancing.

ⓒ She's singing.   ⓓ It's snowing.

18

A: _____

B: He's wearing a brown jacket.

ⓐ What are you doing?

ⓑ What are you wearing?

ⓒ What is he wearing?

ⓓ What is she wearing?

[19-20] Look and write.
그림을 보고 대화의 빈칸에 알맞은 말을 쓰세요.

19

A: What is _____ doing?

B: He's _____ milk.

20

A: What are you _____?

B: _____ wearing green _____.

Let's Go · 3B

2nd Edition

LET'S GO
to the English World

3B

Word Book
& Workbook

CHUNJAE EDUCATION, INC.

Word Book

I Have a Dance Class

Ⓐ Listen and repeat. 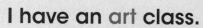 01 02

 **art**
미술

I have an art class.
나는 미술 수업이 있어.

 **computer**
컴퓨터

I have a computer class.
나는 컴퓨터 수업이 있어.

 **dance**
춤, 춤추다

I have a dance class today.
나는 오늘 춤 수업이 있어.

 **ballet**
발레

I have a ballet class today.
나는 오늘 발레 수업이 있어.

 **robot**
로봇

We have a robot class.
우리는 로봇 수업이 있어.

 **reading**
읽기, 독서

We have a reading class.
우리는 읽기 수업이 있어.

 **cooking**
요리

They have a cooking class.
그들은 요리 수업이 있어.

 **badminton**
배드민턴

They have a badminton class.
그들은 배드민턴 수업이 있어.

1 art
미술

2 computer
컴퓨터

3 dance
춤, 춤추다

4 ballet
발레

5 robot
로봇

6 reading
읽기, 독서

7 cooking
요리

8 badminton
배드민턴

Learn More

Monday	월요일	**Tuesday**	화요일	**Wednesday**	수요일
Thursday	목요일	**Friday**	금요일	**Saturday**	토요일
Sunday	일요일				

Ⓐ Listen and repeat. 🎧14 🎧15

breakfast
아침 식사

It's time for breakfast.
아침 식사 할 시간이야.

school
학교

It's time for school.
학교에 갈 시간이야.

class
수업

It's time for class.
수업 들을 시간이야.

lunch
점심 식사

It's time for lunch.
점심 식사 할 시간이야.

dinner
저녁 식사

It's time for dinner.
저녁 식사 할 시간이야.

homework
숙제

It's time for homework.
숙제 할 시간이야.

bed
침대

It's time for bed.
잠자리에 들 시간이야.

B Read, write, and say.

☐Read ☐Write ☐Say

1 breakfast
아침 식사

2 school
학교

3 class
수업

4 lunch
점심 식사

5 dinner
저녁 식사

6 homework
숙제

7 bed
침대

Learn More

time for	~할 시간	It's time for breakfast. 아침 식사 할 시간이야.
late	늦은	We're late. 우리는 늦었어.
Hurry up!	서둘러!	

Ⓐ **Listen and repeat.** 🎧27 🎧28

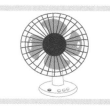

fan
선풍기, 부채

How much is the fan?
선풍기는 얼마예요?

hair band
머리띠

How much is the hair band?
머리띠는 얼마예요?

mask
가면

How much is the mask?
가면은 얼마예요?

storybook
동화책, 이야기책

How much is the storybook?
동화책은 얼마예요?

pencil case
필통

I like this pencil case.
나는 이 필통이 마음에 들어.

teddy bear
곰 인형

I like this teddy bear.
나는 이 곰 인형이 마음에 들어.

board game
보드게임

I want this board game.
나는 이 보드게임을 원해.

soccer ball
축구공

I want this soccer ball.
나는 이 축구공을 원해.

B Read, write, and say.

1 fan
선풍기, 부채

2 hair band
머리띠

3 mask
가면

4 storybook
동화책, 이야기책

5 pencil case
필통

6 teddy bear
곰 인형

7 board game
보드게임

8 soccer ball
축구공

Learn More

how much (값이) 얼마   How much **is it?** 그것은 얼마예요?

dollar 달러 ($)   **It's two** dollars. 그것은 2달러예요.

Line Up, Please

Ⓐ **Listen and repeat.** 🎧40 🎧41

line up
줄을 서다

Line up, **please.**
줄을 서세요.

be quiet
조용히 하다

Be quiet, **please.**
조용히 해 주세요.

wash your hands
손을 씻다

Wash your hands, **please.**
손을 씻으세요.

pick up the trash
쓰레기를 줍다

Pick up the trash, **please.**
쓰레기를 주우세요.

take out the trash
쓰레기를 내다 버리다

Take out the trash, **please.**
쓰레기를 내다 버리세요.

put the bottles here
병을 여기에 넣다

Put the bottles here.
병을 여기에 넣어.

put the paper here
종이를 여기에 넣다

Put the paper here.
종이를 여기에 넣어.

put the cans here
캔을 여기에 넣다

Put the cans here.
캔을 여기에 넣어.

B Read, write, and say.

1 **line up**
줄을 서다

2 **be quiet**
조용히 하다

3 **wash your hands**
손을 씻다

4 **pick up the trash**
쓰레기를 줍다

5 **take out the trash**
쓰레기를 내다 버리다

6 **put the bottles here**
병을 여기에 넣다

7 **put the paper here**
종이를 여기에 넣다

8 **put the cans here**
캔을 여기에 넣다

Learn More

Don't ~.	~하지 마.	Don't **push.** 밀지 마.	
please	~해 주세요 (정중하게 부탁할 때 덧붙이는 말)	**Line up,** please. 줄을 서세요.	

This Hat Is Too Big

A Listen and repeat. 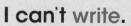 53 54

write
쓰다

I can't write.
나는 쓸 수 없어.

sleep
(잠을) 자다

I can't sleep.
나는 잘 수 없어.

drink
마시다

I can't drink.
나는 마실 수 없어.

run
달리다

I can't run.
나는 달릴 수 없어.

walk
걷다

I can't walk.
나는 걸을 수 없어.

eat
먹다

I can't eat.
나는 먹을 수 없어.

hot
뜨거운

This tea is too hot.
이 차는 너무 뜨거워.

hard
딱딱한

This bed is too hard.
이 침대는 너무 딱딱해.

B Read, write, and say.

☐ Read ☐ Write ☐ Say

1 **write**
쓰다

2 **sleep**
(잠을) 자다

3 **drink**
마시다

4 **run**
달리다

5 **walk**
걷다

6 **eat**
먹다

7 **hot**
뜨거운

8 **hard**
딱딱한

Learn More

short 짧은 ←→ **long** 긴 │ **small** 작은 ←→ **big** 큰 │ **hot** 뜨거운 ←→ **cold** 차가운

A Listen and repeat. 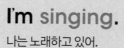 66 67

singing
노래하고 있는

I'm singing.
나는 노래하고 있어.

drawing
(그림을) 그리고 있는

I'm drawing.
나는 그림을 그리고 있어.

studying
공부하고 있는

I'm studying.
나는 공부하고 있어.

cooking
요리하고 있는

I'm cooking.
나는 요리하고 있어.

eating lunch
점심을 먹고 있는

We're eating lunch.
우리는 점심을 먹고 있어.

watching TV
TV를 보고 있는

We're watching TV.
우리는 TV를 보고 있어.

playing the piano
피아노를 치고 있는

They're playing the piano.
그들은 피아노를 치고 있어.

playing the violin
바이올린을 켜고 있는

They're playing the violin.
그들은 바이올린을 켜고 있어.

B **Read, write, and say.**

1 **singing**
노래하고 있는

2 **drawing**
(그림을) 그리고 있는

3 **studying**
공부하고 있는

4 **cooking**
요리하고 있는

5 **eating lunch**
점심을 먹고 있는

6 **watching TV**
TV를 보고 있는

7 **playing the piano**
피아노를 치고 있는

8 **playing the violin**
바이올린을 켜고 있는

Learn More

doing 하고 있는 | **What are you** doing**?** 너는 무엇을 하고 있니?

A Listen and repeat. 79 80

making dinner
저녁 식사를 만들고 있는

I'm making dinner.
나는 저녁 식사를 만들고 있어.

washing the dishes
설거지를 하고 있는

I'm washing the dishes.
나는 설거지를 하고 있어.

cleaning the house
집을 청소하고 있는

He's cleaning the house.
그는 집을 청소하고 있어.

dancing
춤추고 있는

He's dancing.
그는 춤추고 있어.

drinking water
물을 마시고 있는

He's drinking water.
그는 물을 마시고 있어.

sleeping
(잠을) 자고 있는

She's sleeping.
그녀는 자고 있어.

making a robot
로봇을 만들고 있는

She's making a robot.
그녀는 로봇을 만들고 있어.

reading a book
책을 읽고 있는

She's reading a book.
그녀는 책을 읽고 있어.

B Read, write, and say.

1 making dinner
저녁 식사를 만들고 있는

2 washing the dishes
설거지를 하고 있는

3 cleaning the house
집을 청소하고 있는

4 dancing
춤추고 있는

5 drinking water
물을 마시고 있는

6 sleeping
(잠을) 자고 있는

7 making a robot
로봇을 만들고 있는

8 reading a book
책을 읽고 있는

Learn More

dance 춤추다 ⟶ dancing 춤추고 있는

make 만들다 ⟶ making 만들고 있는

He's Wearing a Jacket

Ⓐ Listen and repeat. 92 93

a sweater
스웨터

He's wearing a sweater.
그는 스웨터를 입고 있어.

a skirt
치마

She's wearing a skirt.
그녀는 치마를 입고 있어.

a blouse
블라우스

She's wearing a blouse.
그녀는 블라우스를 입고 있어.

a dress
원피스

She's wearing a dress.
그녀는 원피스를 입고 있어.

a T-shirt
티셔츠

He's wearing a T-shirt.
그는 티셔츠를 입고 있어.

a jacket
재킷

I'm wearing a jacket.
나는 재킷을 입고 있어.

pants
바지

I'm wearing pants.
나는 바지를 입고 있어.

a shirt
셔츠

I'm wearing a shirt.
나는 셔츠를 입고 있어.

Ⓑ Read, write, and say.

1 a sweater
스웨터

2 a skirt
치마

3 a blouse
블라우스

4 a dress
원피스

5 a T-shirt
티셔츠

6 a jacket
재킷

7 pants
바지

8 a shirt
셔츠

Learn More

wearing 입고 있는 | She's wearing a skirt. 그녀는 치마를 입고 있어.

Workbook

Words

A Choose and write.

1

a _____ class

2

a _____ class

3

a _____ class

4

a _____ class

robot

cooking

art

ballet

reading

dance

badminton

computer

5

a _____ class

6

a _____ class

7

a _____ class

8

an _____ class

Practice

(A) Read and mark O or X.

1 I have a ballet class today.

2 I have a cooking class today.

3 I have a badminton class today.

4 I have an art class today.

(B) Circle and write.

1

Fri.

A: It's _____.
(Saturday / Friday)

B: I have _____ today.
(a reading class / a cooking class)

2

Tue.

A: It's _____.
(Tuesday / Thursday)

B: I have _____ today.
(a robot class / a dance class)

Listen & Talk

Ⓐ Read and match.

1 It's Saturday. •

2 It's Thursday. •

3 It's Tuesday. •

4 It's Friday. •

• ⓐ I have a cooking class.

• ⓑ I have a badminton class.

• ⓒ I have an art class.

• ⓓ I have a computer class.

Ⓑ Choose and write.

| Monday   it   ballet   reading   day   Saturday |

1

A: What day is _____ today?

B: It's _____.

I have a _____ class today.

2

A: What _____ is it today?

B: It's _____.

We have a _____ class today.

Write & Talk

A Look and write.

1

A: What _____ is it today?

B: It's _____.

A: I have an _____ class today.

2

A: _____ day is it today?

B: It's _____.

A: I have a _____ class today.

3

A: What day is _____ today?

B: It's _____.

A: We have a _____ class today.

4

A: It's _____.

Do you have a _____ class today?

B: Yes, I _____.

5

A: It's _____.

Do you have a _____ class today?

B: No, I _____.

Story

A Choose and write.

> That's great. | What day is it today? | I have a cooking class.

1

It's Thursday.

2

I can make pizza today.

B Look and write.

1

It's _____.

I have a _____ class today.

2

A: _____ day is it today?

B: It's Monday.

We _____ a _____ class.

3

A: It's _____.

Do you have a _____ class today?

B: _____, I don't.

24

Writing

Ⓐ Make the sentence.

1

| day | today | it | ? | What | is |

....▶ _____

오늘은 무슨 요일이니?

2

| Wednesday | . | It's |

....▶ _____

수요일이야.

3

| badminton | have | . | today | I | a | class |

....▶ _____

나는 오늘 배드민턴 수업이 있어.

4

| a | class | have | . | We | robot | today |

....▶ _____

우리는 오늘 로봇 수업이 있어.

5

| today | an art class | have | you | ? | Do |

....▶ _____

너는 오늘 미술 수업이 있니?

It's Time for School

Words

Ⓐ Look, unscramble, and write.

1

h o s c o l

_____

2

r n e n d i

_____

3

e d b

_____

4

s l a c s

_____

5

t a f a r k e b s

_____

6

n c u h l

_____

7

k r o w o m h e

_____

Practice

(A) Look and check.

1

It's time for ☐ class.
☐ bed.

2

It's time for ☐ lunch.
☐ school.

3

It's time for ☐ homework.
☐ breakfast.

4

It's time for ☐ bed.
☐ dinner.

(B) Circle and write.

> What time is it?

1

It's eight _____. (fifteen / ten)

It's time for _____. (school / bed)

2

It's _____ twenty. (nine / eleven)

It's time for _____. (breakfast / class)

Listen & Talk

A Look and match.

What time is it?

1

2:40

2

8:20

3

12:00

It's twelve o'clock.

It's eight twenty.

It's two forty.

It's time for school.

It's time for lunch.

It's time for class.

B Choose and write.

What time is it?

1

6:15

It's six _____.

It's time for _____.

2

10:30

It's ten _____.

It's time for _____.

3

4:50

It's four _____.

It's time for _____.

| homework | thirty | fifteen | dinner | fifty | bed |

28

Write & Talk

A Look and write.

1

A: What time is _____?

B: It's eight _____.

It's time for _____.

2

A: What _____ is it?

B: It's _____ ten.

It's _____ for lunch.

3

A: _____ time is it?

B: It's five _____.

It's time for _____.

4

A: I'm _____. What time is it?

B: It's six _____.

It's time _____ dinner.

5

A: I'm sleepy. What time _____ it?

B: It's nine _____. It's time for _____.

A: Okay. Good _____.

Story

A Read and number.

| 1 It's time for bed. | 2 It's time for school. | 3 It's time for an art class. |

B Look and write.

1

8:15

A: What time is it?

B: It's eight _____.

It's time for _____.

2

7:00

A: What time is it?

B: It's _____ _____.

It's time _____ _____.

3

11:30

A: What time is it?

B: _____

_____

Writing

Ⓐ Make the sentence.

1

[time] [?] [it] [What] [is]

···▶ _____

몇 시예요?

2

[ten] [four] [.] [It's]

···▶ _____

4시 10분이야.

3

[school] [time] [.] [It's] [for]

···▶ _____

학교에 갈 시간이야.

4

[time] [.] [lunch] [for] [It's]

···▶ _____

점심 식사 할 시간이야.

5

[time] [.] [It's] [for] [bed]

···▶ _____

잠잘 시간이야.

How Much Is It?

Words

Ⓐ Look and write.

1

__tor__b__o__

2

ha__ __ b__n__

3

__o__rd __ __me

4

__ __n

5

p__n__ __l __a__e

6

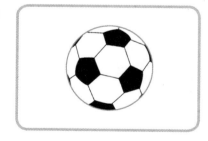

s__c__er __a__l

7

__e__d__ be__r

8

m__ __ __

Practice

A Read and match.

How much is it?

1

$10

It's eight dollars.

It's ten dollars.

2

$4

3

$8

It's five dollars.

It's four dollars.

4

$5

B Choose and write.

two	nine	three
fan	mask	soccer ball

1

$3

A: How much is the _____?

B: It's _____ dollars.

2

$9

A: How much is the _____?

B: It's _____ dollars.

3

$2

A: How much is the _____?

B: It's _____ dollars.

Listen & Talk

A Read and match.

 • $8  • $15  • $9  • $10

1 How much is the storybook? •   • a It's eight dollars.

2 How much is the soccer ball? •   • b It's ten dollars.

3 How much is the pencil case? •   • c It's nine dollars.

4 How much is the teddy bear? •   • d It's fifteen dollars.

B Follow and write.

dollars   want   hair band   much   seven   fan

1  $7

a A: I _____ this mask.
  How _____ is it?
B: It's six dollars.

2  $4

b A: How much is the _____?
B: It's _____ dollars.

3  $6

c A: I like this _____.
  How much is it?
B: It's four _____.

34

Write & Talk

(A) Look and write.

1

A: How much is the _____?

B: It's _____ dollars.

2

A: _____ much is the _____?

B: It's _____ dollars.

A: Here you are.

3

A: Can I _____ you?

B: Yes, please. How much is the _____?

A: It's ten _____.

4

A: _____ I help you?

B: Yes, _____.

How much is the _____?

A: It's _____ dollars.

5

A: I want this _____. How _____ is it?

B: It's _____ dollars.

A: Here _____ are.

Story

A Choose and write.

| How much is the storybook? | I want this teddy bear. | It's five dollars. |

1

How much is it?

_____

2

It's four dollars.

B Look, write, and number in order.

1

$15

☐ It's _____ dollars.

☐ Can I help you?

☐ Yes, please. How much is the _____?

2

$20

☐ Here you are.

☐ I want this _____. How much is it?

☐ It's _____ dollars.

Writing

(A) Make the sentence.

1

| is | How | ? | much | kite | the |

...▶ _____

연은 얼마예요?

2

| the | much | ? | How | is | jump rope |

...▶ _____

줄넘기는 얼마예요?

3

| dollars | . | It's | two |

...▶ _____

그것은 2달러예요.

4

| The | is | . | dollars | storybook | three |

...▶ _____

동화책은 3달러예요.

5

| teddy bear | this | . | I | like |

...▶ _____

저는 이 곰 인형이 마음에 들어요.

Line Up, Please

Words

A Look and match.

1   take out the trash   •

2   pick up the trash   •

3   line up   •

4   be quiet   •

5   put the paper here   •

6   put the cans here   •

7   wash your hands   •

8   put the bottles here   •

Practice

A Look and match.

1
Pick up

2
Wash

3
Line

4
Be

quiet.

the trash.

your hands.

up.

B Choose and write.

cans   paper   bottles

1

A: Put the _____ here.

B: Okay.

2

A: Put the _____ here.

B: Okay.

3

A: Put the _____ here.

B: Okay.

Listen & Talk

A Look and number.

- ◯ Put the bottles here.
- ◯ Pick up the trash.
- ◯ Line up.
- ◯ Put the paper here.

B Choose and write.

> Be quiet
> Wash your hands
> Take out the trash

1

A: _____, please.

B: Okay.

2

A: _____, please.

B: Okay.

3

A: _____, please.

B: Okay. I'm sorry.

Write & Talk

Ⓐ Look and write.

1

A: It's time for lunch.

_____ your _____.

B: Okay.

2

A: _____ the _____ here, please.

B: Okay.

3

A: _____ push.

_____ up, please.

B: _____. I'm sorry.

4

A: Don't _____.

Be _____, please.

B: Okay. I'm _____.

5

A: Don't do that.

_____ up the _____.

B: Okay. _____ sorry.

Story

Ⓐ Read and match.

1

2

3

Ⓐ
A: Pick up the trash, please.

B: Oh, I'm sorry.

ⓑ
A: Line up, please.

B: Okay.

ⓒ
A: Be quiet, please.

B: Okay.

Ⓑ Look and write.

1

A: It's _____ for lunch.

_____ your hands, _____.

B: Okay.

2

A: _____ do that.

Put the _____ _____, please.

B: Okay. I'm _____.

Writing

Ⓐ Make the sentence.

1

the . up Pick trash

····▶ _____

쓰레기를 주워.

2

Line please . up,

····▶ _____

줄을 서세요.

3

please hands, Wash . your

····▶ _____

손을 씻으세요.

4

trash, the out . Take please

····▶ _____

쓰레기를 내다 버리세요.

5

here, Put bottles please . the

····▶ _____

병을 여기에 버리세요.

This Hat Is Too Big

Words

Ⓐ Circle and write.

1

_____

s h o t e r q

2

_____

g h a r d h o

3

_____

m w a l k e t

4

_____

a e a t a t o

5

_____

l e a r u n m

6

_____

c q s l e e p

7

_____

b d r i n k n

8

_____

r w r i t e a

Practice

A Look and check.

1

☐ This tea is too cold.
☐ This tea is too hot.

2

☐ This bed is too big.
☐ This bed is too small.

3

☐ These pants are too long.
☐ These pants are too short.

B Circle and write.

1

This pencil is too _____. (long / short)

I can't _____. (write / walk)

2

These shoes are too _____. (big / small)

I can't _____. (sleep / run)

Listen & Talk

Ⓐ Read and match.

1 This water is too cold.

I can't see.

2 This hat is too big.

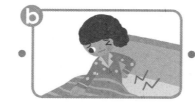

I can't drink it.

3 This bed is too hard.

I can't sleep.

Ⓑ Circle, choose, and write.

pants   pie   hot   walk   long   eat

1

(This / These) _____ is too _____.

I can't _____ it.

2

(This / These) _____ are too _____.

I can't _____.

Write & Talk

(A) **Look and write.**

1

This pencil is _____ short.

I can't _____ .

2

This milk is too _____ .

I _____ drink it.

3

These _____ are _____ hard.

I can't _____ them.

4

A: _____ pants are too _____ .

I _____ run.

B: You need new _____ .

5

A: _____ bed is too _____ .

I can't _____ .

B: Oh, you need a _____ bed.

Story

A Read and match.

1

This bed is too small.

I can't sleep.

2

This pencil is too short.

I can't write.

3

These cookies are too hard.

I can't eat them.

B Look and write.

1

This tea is too _____.

I can't _____ it.

2

These shoes are _____ _____.

I _____ dance.

I need new _____.

Writing

A Make the sentence.

1

is · water · too · . · This · cold

...▶ _____

이 물은 너무 차가워.

2

small · hat · too · This · . · is

...▶ _____

이 모자는 너무 작아.

3

too · pants · . · are · These · short

...▶ _____

이 바지는 너무 짧아.

4

write · . · can't · I

...▶ _____

나는 쓸 수 없어.

5

can't · I · eat · . · them

...▶ _____

나는 그것들을 먹을 수 없어.

What Are You Doing?

Words

A Match and write.

1

_____

5

_____

drawing

singing

2

_____

6

_____

cooking

studying

3

_____

7

_____

watching TV

playing the violin

4

_____

8

_____

eating lunch

playing the piano

Practice

A Read and mark O or X.

1 I'm cooking.

2 I'm watching TV.

3 I'm playing the piano.

4 I'm drawing.

B Match and write.

What are you doing?

1

studying   I'm _____.

2

drawing   I'm _____.

3

singing   I'm _____.

Listen & Talk

(A) Look and number.

What are you doing?

1  2

3  4

( ) I'm studying.

( ) I'm drawing.

( ) I'm cooking.

( ) I'm playing the violin.

(B) Follow, choose, and write.

1

A: What are you doing?

B: I'm _____.

2

A: What are you doing?

B: I'm _____.

3

A: What are you doing?

B: I'm _____.

| watching TV | singing | playing the piano |

Write & Talk

A Look and write.

1

A: What _____ you doing?

B: I'm _____.

2

A: What are you _____?

B: I'm _____ lunch.

3

A: _____ are you?

B: I'm in the living room.

A: _____ are you doing?

B: _____ _____ TV.

4

A: What are _____ doing?

B: I'm _____. I like soup.

5

A: _____ play soccer.

B: Sorry, I _____. I'm busy.

A: What are you _____?

B: I'm _____.

Story

A Circle and write.

1

A: What are you doing?

B: I'm _____.

(eating lunch / watching TV)

2

A: What are you doing?

B: I'm _____.

(cooking / drawing)

3

A: What are you doing?

B: I'm _____.

(studying / playing the piano)

B Look and write.

1

A: What are you _____?

B: I'm _____ _____.

I like pizza.

2

A: Where are _____?

B: I'm _____ the living room.

A: _____ are you doing?

B: I'm _____.

Writing

A Make the sentence.

1

| What | you | doing | are | ? |

...▶ _____

너는 무엇을 하고 있니?

2

| drawing | I'm | . |

...▶ _____

나는 그림을 그리고 있어.

3

| eating | . | I'm | lunch |

...▶ _____

나는 점심을 먹고 있어.

4

| violin | the | . | I'm | playing |

...▶ _____

나는 바이올린을 켜고 있어.

5

| basketball | . | play | Let's |

...▶ _____

농구를 하자.

Words

A Look and check.

1

- [ ] drawing
- [ ] dancing

2

- [ ] drinking water
- [ ] reading a book

3

- [ ] cleaning the house
- [ ] making dinner

4

- [ ] eating lunch
- [ ] washing the dishes

5

- [ ] reading a book
- [ ] watching TV

6

- [ ] singing
- [ ] sleeping

7

- [ ] drinking water
- [ ] making a robot

8

- [ ] making dinner
- [ ] washing the dishes

Practice

A Look and match.

1

He's — sleeping.

She's — dancing.

2

He's — making a robot.

She's — making dinner.

3

He's — reading a book.

She's — drinking water.

B Circle and write.

1

A: What is _____ doing? (he / she)

B: He's _____.

(making dinner / reading a book)

2

A: What is _____ doing? (he / she)

B: She's _____.

(washing the dishes / drinking water)

Listen & Talk

Ⓐ Look, write, and match.

1

What is _____ doing?

2

What is _____ doing?

3

What is _____ doing?

He's sleeping.

She's drinking milk.

She's making a robot.

Ⓑ Choose and write.

She's	What	doing
cleaning	dancing	dinner

1

A: What is he _____?

B: He's _____.

2

A: What is Mom doing?

B: _____ making _____.

3

A: _____ is Dad doing?

B: He's _____ the bathroom.

Write & Talk

A Look and write.

1

A: What is _____ doing?

B: She's _____ .

2

A: What is _____ doing?

B: He's _____ water.

3

A: Where is Andy?

B: He's in the _____ .

A: He's _____ the _____ .

4

A: _____ is Kelly?

B: She's _____ the bedroom.

She's _____ a book.

5

A: Where _____ Mom?

B: _____ in the living room.

A: _____ is she doing?

B: She's _____ the house.

Story

A Choose and write.

| What is Amy doing? | What are you doing? | I'm washing the dishes. |

1

2

She's playing with Max.

B Look and write.

1

A: What is _____ doing?

B: He's _____.

2

A: What is _____ doing?

B: He's _____.

3

A: Emily is _____ the bedroom.

B: What is _____ doing?

A: She's _____.

Writing

Ⓐ Make the sentence.

1

| she | What | doing | is | ? |

┈┈▶ _____

그녀는 무엇을 하고 있니?

2

| doing | ? | Tony | What | is |

┈┈▶ _____

토니는 무엇을 하고 있니?

3

| making | He's | . | dinner |

┈┈▶ _____

그는 저녁을 만들고 있어.

4

| the | He's | . | house | cleaning |

┈┈▶ _____

그는 집을 청소하고 있어.

5

| kitchen | in | . | She's | the |

┈┈▶ _____

그녀는 부엌에 있어.

Words

Ⓐ Follow, choose, and write.

a blouse	a T-shirt	a dress
a jacket	a skirt	a sweater
a shirt	pants	

1 [　　　　] 2 [　　　　] 3 [　　　　] 4 [　　　　]

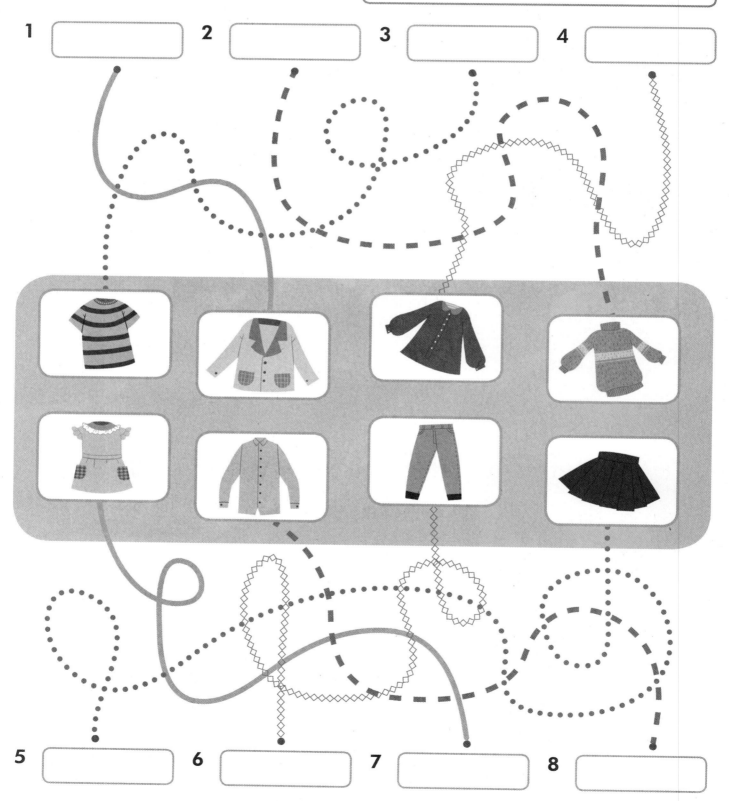

5 [　　　　] 6 [　　　　] 7 [　　　　] 8 [　　　　]

Practice

Ⓐ Read and choose.

1 She's wearing a blouse.

   Ⓐ   Ⓑ

2 He's wearing a T-shirt.

   Ⓐ   Ⓑ

3 He's wearing a shirt.

   Ⓐ   Ⓑ

4 She's wearing a skirt.

   Ⓐ   Ⓑ

Ⓑ Circle and write.

1

A: What is (he / she) wearing?

B: (He's / She's) wearing _____.

                     (a dress / a sweater)

2

A: What is (he / she) wearing?

B: (He's / She's) wearing _____.

                     (a jacket / pants)

Listen & Talk

A Read and write T or F.

1

A: What is he wearing?

B: He's wearing a blue shirt.

2

A: What is she wearing?

B: She's wearing green pants.

3

A: What is she wearing?

B: She's wearing a red blouse.

4

A: What are you wearing?

B: I'm wearing a white T-shirt.

B Choose and write.

| skirt | wearing | he |
| sweater | What | She's |

1 A: What is she _____?

B: _____ wearing a pink _____.

2 A: _____ is _____ wearing?

B: He's wearing a yellow _____.

Write & Talk

Ⓐ Look and write.

1

A: What are _____ wearing?

B: I'm wearing a _____.

2

blue

A: _____ is he wearing?

B: He's wearing blue _____.

3

white

A: What is she _____?

B: She's wearing a white _____.

4

brown

A: That's my brother.

B: What is _____ wearing?

A: He's wearing a _____ _____.

5

yellow

red

A: That's my sister.

B: What is _____ wearing?

A: She's wearing a yellow _____ and

a red _____.

Story

Ⓐ Read and write the letter.

ⓐ a red jacket	ⓑ a white jacket	ⓒ a white hat	ⓓ red pants

1

A: What is he wearing?

B: He's wearing ☐ and ☐.

2

A: What is she wearing?

B: She's wearing ☐ and ☐.

Ⓑ Look and write.

1 A: What is he wearing?

B: He's wearing a _____ _____.

He's _____ black _____, too.

2 A: What is she wearing?

B: She's wearing a _____ _____.

_____ wearing a yellow _____, too.

Writing

A Make the sentence.

1

| What | you | ? | are | wearing |

⋯▸ _____

너는 무엇을 입고 있니?

2

| she | ? | is | wearing | What |

⋯▸ _____

그녀는 무엇을 입고 있니?

3

yellow

| a | sweater | . | wearing | He's | yellow |

⋯▸ _____

그는 노란색 스웨터를 입고 있어.

4

green

| green | . | a | She's | dress | wearing |

⋯▸ _____

그녀는 초록색 원피스를 입고 있어.

5

blue

| wearing | hat | a | . | blue | He's |

⋯▸ _____

그는 파란색 모자를 쓰고 있어.